Basilica of the
Sagrada Familia

Texts: Jordi Bonet i Armengol
Cover: Sergi Gómez.
Layout: Eduard Busquets
Photos: Archive, Sagrada Família
Exterior photographs: E. Busquets, C. Socias, J.C. Castañeda, J. Peiró, S. Gómez
English translation: M. Joyce McFarlane
Acknowledgements: Junta de Obras del Templo de la Sagrada Família
Architectural work ©Junta Constructora del Temple de la Sagrada Familia
Archive material ©Junta Constructora del Temple de la Sagrada Familia

Distributed by: CEDOSA
cedosa@cedosa.net

22Dep. Legal: B-11.239-2011

© C.I.F. A08187056

GEOCOLOR

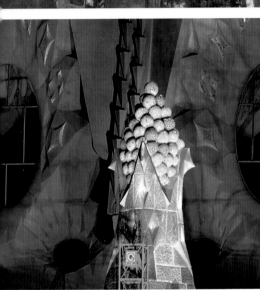

The historical setting

The Sagrada Família is the product of the circumstances stemming from its foundation, and the unique drive of Antoni Gaudí, its architect, who devoted more than 40 years of his life to its building.

The Catholic faith, which had a strong presence in the origins of the Catalan nation in the 10th century, again played a

First project by the architect Francesc de Paula Villar.

Gaudí at the first reading of the poem 'Canigó'.

leading role in the movement leading to the nation's rebirth – the 'Renaixença' or Renaissance - one thousand years later, when workers, farmers and intellectuals, amongst them the country-born priest and poet Jacint Verdaguer, restored their language to its rightful dignity.

The expansion of the city of Barcelona, with the industrial revolution and the impulse of the bourgeoisie, brought into being a powerful capital city

Saint Josep Manyanet.

where art flourished alongside trade and the economy.

Catalonia once again opened up to the world, generously spreading its particular genius far and wide.

At a difficult moment for the Universal Church a Barcelona book-seller, Josep Maria Bocabella, created the Spiritual Association of the Devotees of St. Joseph to give spiritual and material aid to the Holy See, proposing, moreover, to build a monumental church dedicated to the Holy Family ('Sagrada Família'). It would be surrounded by gardens, and respectable public leisure activities would be complemented by learning, education and spiritual contemplation. It was this same devotion to the Holy Family that inspired one of the project's founding fathers, St. Josep Manyanet.

First drawing by Antoni Gaudí in neo-Gothic style.

The Founder, Josep M. Bocabella.

Start of the works.

Founding and cornerstone

On 19 March 1882, the feast of Saint Joseph, the first stone was blessed by the Bishop of Barcelona, Josep Maria Urquinaona i Bidot, assisted by the Bishop Elect of Vic, Josep Morgades and other members of the clergy. Among the other dignitaries present were Josep Maria Bocabella and Manuel de Dalmases, representing the Spiritual Association of the Devotees of St. Joseph. There was also a large gathering of the faithful 'for the greater honour and glory of the Holy Family, to arouse the tepid hearts from their slumbers. Exalt the Faith. Stir up Charity. Invoke the Lord to have mercy on this Country, impelled by its Catholic roots, to think, preach and practise the virtues'.

The walls of the crypt were already under way when due to disagreements with the Devotees of St. Joseph, the architect and author of the project resigned. In November 1883 a promising new architect, Antoni Gaudí i Cornet, was commissioned to carry out the work.

Gaudí, architect of the Sagrada Família

Antoni Gaudí, born on 26 June 1852, was baptised in the Church of Saint Peter in Reus, then Catalonia's second city. The future architect's family were coppersmiths who struggled to give the young Gaudí an education. Reus was a dynamic, prosperous provincial city which, in the space of just a few years, produced other men of great renown. These included Joan Prim, the general who became president of the Spanish government, and Marià Fortuny, a painter famous throughout Europe in the latter third of the 19th century.

Gaudí had obtained his degree in architecture from the Barcelona School of Architecture in 1878. He soon distinguished himself in his chosen field, receiving commissions from the man who would become his friend and patron, Eusebi Güell i Bacigalupi, as well as from the prestigious architect Joan Martorell, who involved him in the Sagrada Família project. He was also friendly with the poet Joan Maragall, the project's main sponsor.

Antoni Gaudí Cornet.

Interior of the architect's studio, exhibition of maquettes, original drawing by Gaudí of the Passion façade, and interior of the store.

Description

A general idea

'In the Sagrada Família, everything is providential' (Gaudí).

A very significant donation received shortly after the crypt was opened for worship (1892) allowed more ambitious work to be carried out on the church and gave Gaudí the chance to develop his creative skills. The conception of the building as a pyramid-shaped volume was exchanged for another with 18 bell-towers or domes, eight of which have now been built on the Nativity and Passion façades.

The church has a basilical ground plan in the form of a Latin cross with a central nave and four side naves, and a transept with a nave and two aisles. The interior of the church is 90 metres in length and 60 metres wide. The central nave is 15 metres wide and the apse is delimited by seven chapels and two circular staircases, with an ambulatory around the presbytery. The building is surrounded by a cloister which links its three great fronts or façades: on the east side, the Nativity, on the west, the Passion and on the south, the Glory. The Glory façade, which faces seawards, is currently under construction. On ei-

Gaudí's drawing of the whole church (1902).

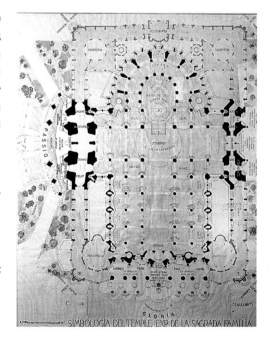

General floorplan of the Basilica with its symbolism and dedication.

SIMBOLOGIA DEL TEMPLE EXP DE LA SAGRADA FAMÍLIA

...ying of the first stone.

The Sagrada Família in 1897.

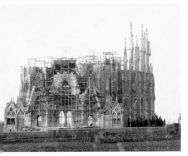

...898

Christmas 1904

1908

...910 with the school.

1913

1925

1926

1928

...930

1936 (destruction)

1963

1972

1983

1993

ther side of the apse are two buildings, the sacristies, which will be used for diocesan administration and parish services. A 170-metre high dome will rise over the centre of the transept, representing Jesus Christ, flanked by another four symbolising the Evangelists. Covering the apse will be another dome, dedicated to Our Lady. Inside, over the side naves are tribunes which along with the apse can be used by a choir of 1,200 singers, whose voices will join those of the faithful. The church will accommodate a total of 10,000 people.

A great inner space of 900 square metres supported by four central columns occupies the centre of the transept, which will have a maximum height of 60 metres. The apse is closed by an immense 75-metre high hyperboloid presided over by the figure of God the Creator. The overhanging porticos are embellished with iconographies of the Nativity, the Passion and the Glory, each crowned by four bell-towers symbolising the twelve Apostles. Each col-

Nativity Façade.

*The apse of the Basilica, keystone
75 m above the presbytery. >*

12

umn is dedicated to an apostle or to one of the Catalan or Spanish dioceses or those of the five continents, with their founding saints, in a synthesis of the universal nature of the Church and its extending from East to West, as the first bishop of Tarragona, St. Fructuosus, prayed for at the moment of his martyrdom.

Conscious that the church would be a work of centuries, Gaudí successfully proposed to the Devotees of St. Joseph that he should complete one façade, the Nativity, so that their own generation could see part of the work finished, serving as a stimulus for its continuity.

Terminations of the windows.

Windows in the cloister.

Terminations of the bell-towers.

A new architecture

Gaudí was a great observer of nature. Always aware of the great importance of the forms and laws of nature, he soon realised that these could also be used in architecture. These forms are often geometric and employ the double curve, making them extra strong. Generated by bundles of straight lines, they include the hyperbolic paraboloid, the hyperboloid, the conoid and the helicoid. As a rule, in nature there is no such thing as discontinuity, moving smoothly from one surface to an-

Interior of the Basilica of the Sagrada Família.

Plaster model of the naves. (scale 1:10).

Light plays a vital role in Gaudí's architecture.

Direct or inverted hyperboloid intersections which form the vaults.

Part of the lighting is integrated into the columns.

Part of the lighting is integrated into the columns.

other. Supporting elements like columns, and supported elements like lintels, acting through the capital, often with a plant (acanthus leaf) or geometric decoration, tend to provide continuity. Gaudí also noticed that walking sticks are not used vertically but are inclined. So why not have leaning columns? He also considered the essential function of the skeleton. He was a great rationalist, in the sense that he did nothing unless it had a rational response: for example, a bone is a cylinder in which the ends (joints) become hyperboloids. In

Colonia Güell

Tree-shaped columns in
the church of the Sagrada Família.

this way he hoped to create a living architecture, an architecture with those cardinal signs of life: colour and movement. One example is his bench for the Park Güell: colour and movement expressed in a neo-Doric cornice.

An architecture which is the synthesis of form and structure, expressed through geometry.

For years, Gaudí took this approach in all his other work so he could bring to the church of the Sagrada Família the best results of his experiments. The commission he received from his friend and patron, Eusebi Güell, for the chapel in his factory at Santa Coloma de Cervelló served as a laboratory for developing these ideas, and he took ten years to produce a satisfactory project. His ideas ranged from structural calculation with the inverted funicular model, to the use of surfaces governed by 'timbrel vault' technology, long a Mediterranean tradition, and actively conserved in Catalonia where it was known as the 'volta catalana' (Catalan vault).

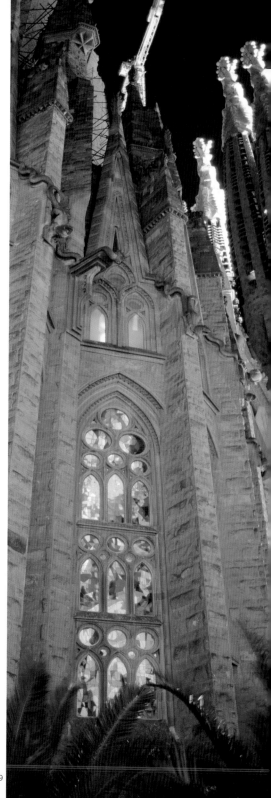

Night-time image of the exterior enhanced by the effects of the interior lighting shining through the stained glass windows.

The Crypt

True to the commission as received, Gaudí maintained the neo-Gothic style of architect Joan Villar, his predecessor on the project, but introduced some changes. He changed the position of the entrance stairway and crowned the vault that covered it with a strikingly beautiful representation of the 'Annunciation of Mary' on the keystone. He also put in windows to light up the space above the ambulatory which surrounds it and separates it from the chapels. He constructed a deep ditch around the crypt to prevent dampness, also raising the central vault to let in natural light. The central chapel of the seven absidal chapels is devoted to the worship of St. Joseph, with the Sacred Heart and the Blessed Virgin on either side accompanied by the remaining members of the Holy Family of Jesus. The altar of St. Joseph was consecrated for worship in 1885.

The crypt is where the life of the parish goes on. Its high altar occupies the central space nearest the transept. On one side stands the Holy Sacrament, and on the other the image of the Virgin of Montserrat is venerated. A mosaic portraying vines and wheat runs around the perimeter of the paved floor. In the chapels at the far ends of the ambulatory are the graves of the Dalmases i Bocabella family (the Holy

Central nave of the crypt.

Keystone portraying the Annunciation.

‹ *Details of the presbytery and chapels: St. Joseph, del Carme with Gaudí's grave, and the Holy Christ.*

Gaudí designed and made some of the liturgical elements of the crypt with his own hands: the lectern and the holder for the Paschal candle.

Christ) and the architect Gaudí himself (Our Lady of Carmen).

Following its destruction in 1936 the entire crypt was restored, including the stained glass windows, the furnishings and all the liturgical elements, which were designed by Gaudí.

The Apse

The apse, built between 1891 and 1895, is neo-Gothic in style, though it contains elements where Gaudí's personality clearly stands out. It consists of seven polygonal-shaped chapels dedicated to the suffering and joy of St. Joseph. At the crown are the antiphones of Advent, beginning with the 'O', with stained glass windows by artist Joan Vila Grau.

The layout of the windows, the contrast of light and shade in the chapels and, especially, the gargoyles and bell-towers of the pinnacles, take their inspiration from the flora and fauna which lived around the building itself: lizards, snails and sea-snails, salamanders, frogs and tadpoles. Larger than life-sized representations of plants constitute an extraordinary natural-ist vision at the service of architecture.

The buttresses separating the chapels are adorned by images of the Founding Saints.

These days, the central chapel and the ambulatory are used for worship. The central part is raised some 2 metres above the church's floor and occupies the pres-bytery, accommodating three hundred clerics.

The high altar is set between two columns dedicated to the apostles St. Peter and St.

Snakes, snails and lizards form part of the gargoyles and decorative elements of the walls of the absidal chapels.

The vault capping the apse is a great hyperboloid.

Paul. It consists of a great block of porphyry covered by a heptagonal baldaquin 5 m in diameter which portrays the seven gifts of the Holy Spirit. Following the description given by Gaudí, 50 hanging lamps have been placed here, decorated with the Eucharistic symbols of ears of corn and grapes. The Holy Christ inspired by the figure commissioned by Gaudí from the sculptor Carles Mani is set right in the middle, with a white tapestry canopy symbolising God the Father.

Presbytery with altar, pulpit and porphyry bishop's throne.

Throne, choir stalls and organ framed by the stained glass windows.

Choir stalls fill the space presided over by the bishop's throne, and visible at the back of the apse, the pipes of the organ form a symmetrical backcloth. The space above rises to a height of 75 m in a great hyperboloid of some 18 m in diameter, constructed using the 'timbrel vault' technology. Of particular note is the blue of the 'trencadís' mosaic of Venetian glass, with a large image at its centre, a great golden triangle symbolising God the Father, the Creator, visible from the main portal thanks to the geometry that conforms and defines it.

'Inside the vault of the dome of Our Lady... which will be visible on entering the church, ... the Eternal Father, whose vestments, ... vision of the prophet who says that the vestments of the Father fill the whole of the heavens, will cover the whole of the dome' (text of the 1926 Album on the Sagrada Família, published by the Devotees of St. Joseph).

A dome which will eventually be covered by a luminous crown of twelve stars will rise to a height of 120 m around the completed interior vault.

Corbels, columns and play of light in the interior.

Rose Tree Door (1899). >

The Cloister

The arrangement of the cloister, encircling the church, is very different from that usually found in basilicas, monasteries or cathedrals. The cloister which is interrupted by doors, chapels and sacristies, allows processions to pass through and separates the church from outside noise. The lower ground floor has spaces which can be used as workshops, services or storerooms .

Initially, Gaudí built the first two stretches on either side of the Nativity façade, placing doors dedicated to Our Lady of the Rose Tree and Our Lady of Montserrat in the irregular space between the bell-towers. These portals cover conical lanterns through which the daylight enters.

In order to show what could be done, Gaudí completed the section dedicated to Our Lady of the Rose Tree with extraordinary craftsmanship. This is filigree work which reminds one of needlepoint or fine basket-weaving, surrounded by roses and rose trees. Our Lady of the Rose Tree with the Child presides over the archivolt of the portal, along with St. Dominic and St. Catherine of Siena. On either side of the portal are the Patriarchs, Kings and Prophets, Isaac, Jacob, David and Solomon. On the corbels of the vault groins are representations of the Death of the Righteous

Decorative details of walls and corbels on the keystone.

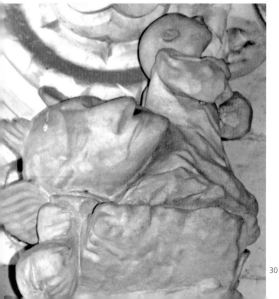

and the Temptations of Mankind. The text of the Ave Maria invites the faithful to make the angelic salutation, whilst the words '*Et in hora mortis nostrae, Amen*' give significance to the company of Jesus, Joseph and Mary as comfort to the dying. The temptations are expressed as the devil placing a bomb in the hands of a terror-

Temptation of woman.

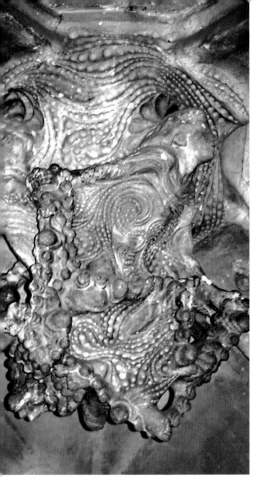

Angelic figures

ist, and with a purse with which he prostitutes women.

Part of the sections at each side leading to the Passion façade have been constructed, those dedicated to the Our Lady of Mercy and Our Lady of Sorrows, and along with the sculptural decoration are awaiting completion.

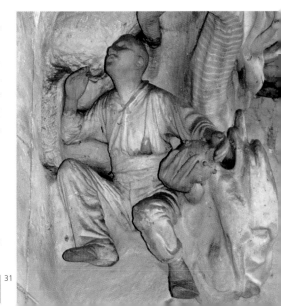

Temptation of man

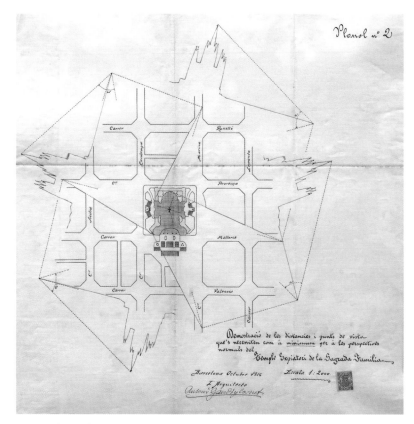

Surroundings of the church with silhouettes and layout of square signed by Gaudí.

Nativity Façade. >

The Façades

Gaudí proposed to build the Nativity façade with the idea that his own generation should see it completed. This was a challenge for the continuation of the work, so that future generations too would terminate parts of the church, whose construction would necessarily extend over a long period. The east and west façades have three doors symbolising the theological virtues of Faith, Hope and Charity. They are crowned by four bell-towers repre-

senting the Apostles. On these can be read the words *Sanctus, Sanctus, Sanctus i Hosanna Excelsis.* It was Gaudí's wish that all, on reading this inscription, would praise the Lord.

Nativity Façade

In the central archivolt under the Star of the Orient are set Jesus, Mary and Joseph, between the ox and the mule, and surrounded by singing angels. On either side are the Adoration of the Shepherds and the Magi. Higher up, angels play trumpets

Betrothal of Joseph and Mary.

Coronation of Mary.

Presentation of Jesus at the temple.

Angels.

announcing the Nativity. The Annunciation and the Coronation of Mary are still higher. Finally there is a cypress tree, the refuge of birds, symbolising the Church as a huge bell-tower crowned by a 'Tau', the Greek initial letter of the name of God. On the south side, around the Door of Hope, is the Betrothal of Joseph and Mary, the Flight to Egypt, the Massacre of the Innocents, the ship of the Church steered by Joseph and, on the bell-tower, a rock of Montserrat inscribed with the word **'Salveu-nos'** ('Save us'). On the other side is the Door of Faith, with representations of the Visitation, Christ amongst the Doctors, the Presentation in the Temple and Jesus the Worker at his carpenter's bench. On the pinnacles are ears of wheat and grapes, with the image of Mary in the dogma of the Blessed Virgin.

< Nativity on a column with the genealogy of Jesus.

Passion Façade

Desolation, relinquishment, pain, sacrifice and death provide the counterpoint on the west front, which is presided over by the death of Christ so that his Resurrection and Ascension into Heaven can be proclaimed from the heights. The portal was planned by Gaudí after 1911, when ill and in pain in Puigcerdà, he had time on his hands to study and meditate upon it. 'I am ready', he said, 'to sacrifice the building itself, to smash vaults and cut columns in order to give an idea of the cruelty of the sacrifice'.

The sculptor Josep Maria Subirachs created around 100 figures evoking the Passion of Christ, beginning with the figure of Christ at the Column on the mullion of

Passion Façade.

Christ crucified.

Scourging at the Pillar.

the central portal. Alone, the figure of Jesus bound is flanked on either side by the Betrayal of Judas and the Denial of Peter. Above, the Via Dolorosa, with Jesus carrying the Cross after being condemned by Pilate. The figure of Veronica is at the centre, showing the image of the 'Man of Sorrow, the imprint of a face, enveloped in mystery. The figures of Mary, St. John, the Holy Women, the soldiers and the people lead up to the scene of the Holy Sepulchre. The image of Christ Resurrected ascending to Heaven between the bell-towers will complete the representation of the human life of Christ in the catechistic vision of the Mystery of our Salvation.

The construction of the great dome and pediment planned by Gaudí, with the 18 columns created by a combination of hyperbolic paraboloids, is at last under way. This is the result of a long exercise of research into the use of computer software to cut these shapes, which although different are very similar. Subirachs has created the figures of the Lion of Juda and the Lamb of Isaac which will be located at the extremes of this façade. Within them are the names of the patriarchs and prophets, and between the bell-towers and the façade, as Gaudí wished, will be the empty tomb.

From inside the church the stained glass window of the Resurrection is like an ex-

Kiss of Judas.

The trial of Jesus. Pilate washes his hands.

The Ascension, gilded bronze figure.

Road to Calvary and the death of Jesus.

plosion of light which reveals the Resuscitated Christ, work of Joan Vila Grau.

*The Veil of
· Veronica.*

Original model of the study of volumes for the Glory Façade and a modern plaster model.

Glory Façade

Gaudí left a study of the volumes and structure and iconographic and symbolic design of this main façade, which faces seawards. A monumental narthex gives way to three portals and is crowned by four bell-towers flanked on either side by the chapel of the sacrament and the baptistry. There are eleven doors leading directly or through the cloister into the chapels, and from these into the church itself.

The central portal has three doors. The narthex is covered by the vaults which support the bell-towers, 16 lanterns and some hyperboloids. These asymmetrical hyperboloids extend and crown a series of cones. The whole forms a grandiose tympanum with ascending hyperboloids, in which Gaudí envisioned an iconographic representation of the *Gloria*.

Stony clouds are inscribed with the symbol of Faith, the '*Credo*'. The entrance, at the same level as the entire church, is high enough above Carrer Mallorca to allow the road to run below it, and the narthex opens out into a great open

Main portal in the Glory Façade.

space. On either side, Gaudí imagined a 20-metre high waterspout and a huge flaming cresset: purifying fire and water. The iconography presents Man within the Order of Creation, his origin and his end, with the Way to achieve it. Since Adam and Eve, through hard work and by practising virtue man can conquer the Glory which Christ opened for us through the Redemption and with the help of Grace. We also find the Beatitudes, the Virtues and the Cardinal Sins: Hell is represented beneath the vaults. Higher up is Purgatory and over each of the seven doors, representing the Sacraments, is a prayer to Our Father.

In the centre of the façade is St. Joseph at work, with the attributes of the manual trades. Higher up, Mary presides as a Queen over the Saints, whilst at the top is Christ with the attributes of the Passion and the seven trumpeting angels announcing the Last Judgement. All the angel hierarchies surround the Eternal Father and, in the large central rose window, the Holy Spirit completes this vision of the Trinity.

Subirachs has made bronze doors for the central portal, with the Lord's Prayer and the sentence 'Give us this day our daily bread' in 50 languages.

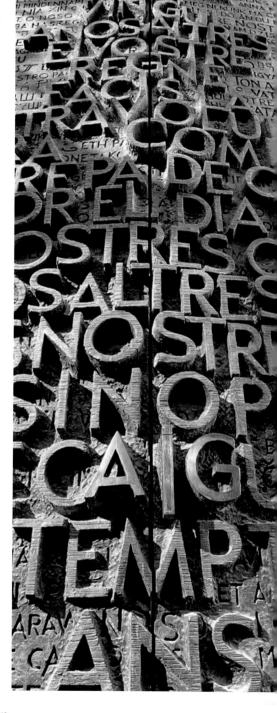

Detail.

The Naves

The naves are made up of completely new forms with original geometric solutions and structures. They are the result of years of study and reflection. Gaudí began the project for the naves around 1910, incorporating his experience with the chapel of the Colonia Güell. A solution with slightly helicoidal columns, arches and vaults with hyperbolic paraboloids was published in 1917. The discovery of the luminous quality of hyperboloids led Gaudí to use them in the central nave, in a transept of concave-convex domes, interspersing columns with walls and high windows. The forms, of which 1:10 models were made, constitute a vision of the forest which the architect often used as an image to explain his project. These columns, vaults, high windows and roofs form what Gaudí considered the final result of the design work, and the overall and structural lines of this definitive design were presented by his assistant, Sugrañes, in 1923 to the Catalan Association of Architects. In recent years this 1:10 scale model has been constructed to Gaudí's design, achieving the continuity of forms as they exist in nature.

Columns, vaults and stained glass windows evoke a luminous wood.

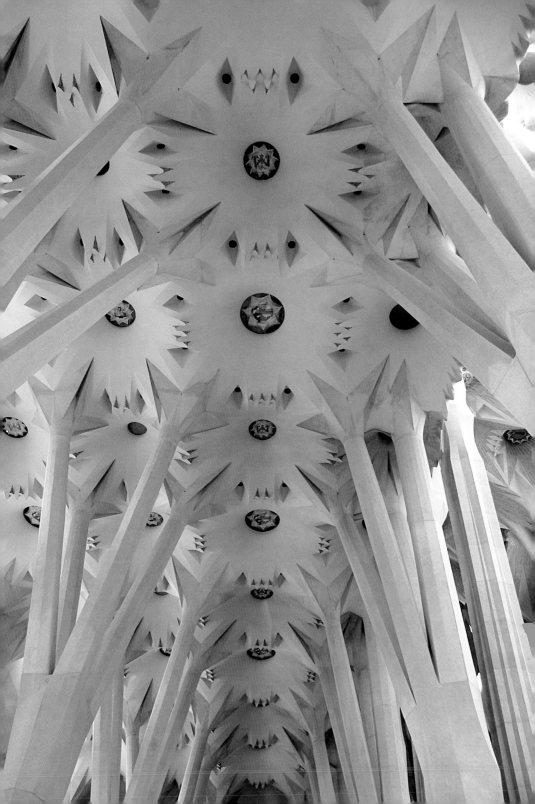

The Columns

In itself, this new solution for vertical support conceived by Gaudí, leaning slightly 'so as to follow the pressure curve supporting the weight of the roof' is an extraordinary creative innovation. The intersection of two helicoids produces arrises, which originate in the concave sections of the starred polygon at the base, multiplying as they twist upwards.

The first twist occurs at a height in metres equal to the number of sides in the base polygon. The second begins at a height equal to half the number of sides, producing twice as many new arrises. The third twist, at a height of one quarter of the number of sides of the polygon, quadruples the number of arrises. In this way, then, at a height in metres that is double the number of sides of the base, the arrises multiply and the polygon turns into a circle. Gaudí's column is at once both extraordinary and simple. It produces arrises which become finer and multiply as the column rises, springing from the deepest parts of each groove. As the column ascends, it combines the lightness of helicoidal growth with the gravity of the Doric column.

This is a startling, wholly new column of exceptional beauty. It will come as no sur-

Tree-shaped columns.

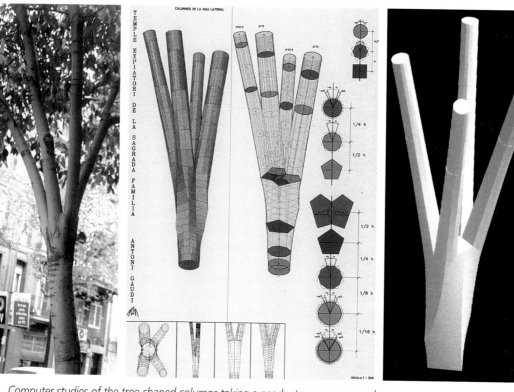

COLUMNES DE LA NAU LATERAL

1/4 h

1/2 h

1/2 h

1/4 h

1/8 h

1/16 h

ESCALA I : 200

Computer studies of the tree-shaped columns taking a nearby tree as an example.

prise to learn that Gaudí planned to use it throughout the church, but with varying polygons. The first was a starred octagon. In the naves it was a hexagon, a square and a pentagon, a rectangle, a decahedron and a dodecahedron. Gaudí played with these shapes, inverted them, twisted them, achieving in architectural form the arboreal vision he obtained from observing the trees outside his studio.

Columns. Detail of the capitals.

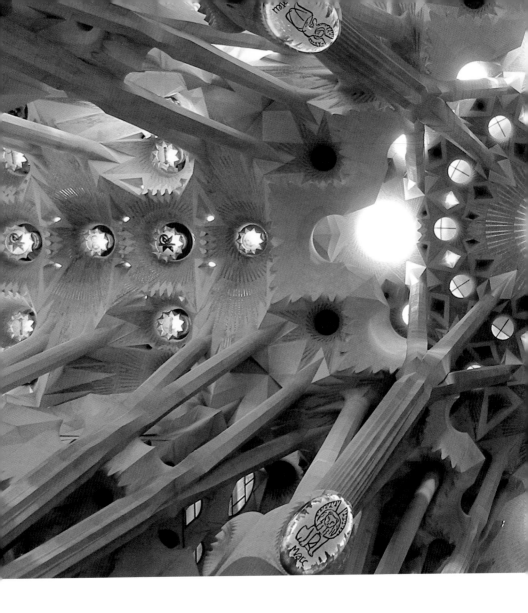

The Vaults

Set on the lower parts of the columns are knots or capitals, large elements that generate new columns which reach up like branches to the vaults. Their inclination follows the lines of pressure and reduces light in the vaults. The solid or empty hyperboloids which form them are interwoven together in the shape of stars. They form a taut, light structure which, as seen in the original 1:10 scale model, in other words only the plaster, is in itself one of the achievements which best establishes Gaudí's lasting contribution to 20th-century architecture.

Tree-shaped columns and vaults.

The vaults house the central lamps on the cinctures of the hyperboloids, rich in symbols and figurations, with anagrams of Jesus, Mary and Joseph. In the crossing, three concentric circles of hyperboloids intertwined with hyperbolic paraboloids fill the space with light, which glides over the Venetian gold mosaic. Two circles of twelve hyperboloids symbolise the 24 Elders of the Apocalypse, and in the centre, at a height of 66 m, is the figure which represents Jesus Christ, with a cincture 4 m in diameter. In future, as Gaudí planned it, a great chandelier will hang there representing the celestial Jerusalem, with the twelve towers around it, according to the vision of St. John.

Detail of the well of one of the lifts and the stairs.

Side nave, vault.

Finally, a great 14 m paraboloid links the crossing and the apse with angelic figures, making up the dome of the sky which forms the cloak of God the Father, Almighty Creator, whose centre is light and the Trinity, the decoration that Gaudí imagined.

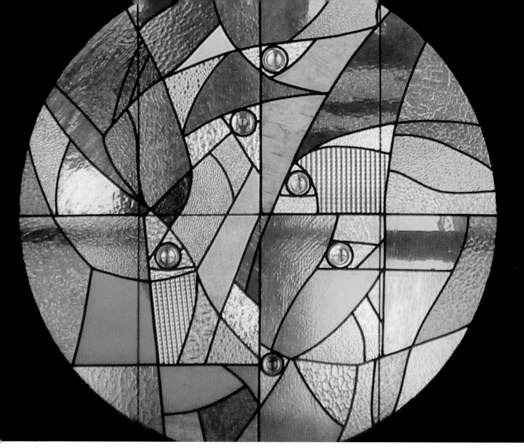

Rose window.

The Windows

All down the nave and the transept are graceful windows allowing light to filter in through geometrical forms begun in the neo-Gothic side of the Nativity façade, then changing into paraboloids, revolving and flat hyperboloids which, as Gaudí put it, 'make mouldings unnecessary, since light enters and is diffused in a play of varying intensity and colour'. Externally they are decorated with the fruits of every season, following the cycle of the year and symbolising the fruit rained down on all mankind by the Holy Spirit. On the mullion above each window is a Founding Saint: Ignatius of Loyola, Joseph of Calasanz, Vincent de Paul, Philip Neri, Peter Nolasco, Anthony Mary Claret, Joaquima Vedruna, John Bosco, Joan of Lestonnac and Josep Manyanet.

Terminating each of these windows are baskets brimming with all kinds of fruit, representing good works carried out.

Original model of the roof in the central nave.

up the transept and the altar, exalting the entire church', said Gaudí, 'culminating the pyramidising of the building'.

During his last years' continuous work on the church, Gaudí had completed the structural study of the building, of which all we know are a number of sketches showing a similar structure to that of the sacristies, though longer, with an octagonal cross-section rounded off by concave paraboloids The great height is divided up into twelve or thirteen storeys, with small columns and a sturdy double shell and the use of unfaced brick and stone on the exterior. The ciborium of Our Lady covers the apse, which is so wide that it looks like a dome.

The roof of the central nave is formed by pyramids, one per section, interconnected and linked to the front of the windows with large paraboloids. Some aediculae bearing the anagrams of the Holy Family support and crown lanterns 70 metres high with the words *'Al.leluia, Amen'*, on parabolic shields.

The space between the vaults and the roof is divided horizontally into four storeys supported by clusters of four inclined columns which rise above the upper ramifications of the main columns. The side naves are covered by barely sloping surfaces featuring beautifully finished pyra-

The Roofs

Their verticality makes these one of the unique elements in the entire church, despite their functionality (to protect the church from the rain and other elements). 'A monumental unit of six domes lights

Detail of the upper part of the cloister beside the baptistry.

Eucharistic symbols of bread and wine.

mid-shaped lanterns illuminating the top storey and diffusing the light.

The outer layer of the roof was to be weather-resistant stone from Montjuïc. With structural supports - floors and colonnades and the vaults making up the interior - Gaudí's basic premise is ever-present: 'Divide the inert loads and multiply the active elements'.

Current regulations require the use of reinforced concrete in the structure, but the Master insisted on the need for double roofs in such singular buildings, indicating that ceramic and stone had to be used, as

Roof of the Rose Tree pinnacle.

in other buildings like Casa Batlló, Belles-guard and La Pedrera.

So the roofs were built without steel. No-one is sure how long this technology will last - it is less than a century old and may cause serious maintenance problems in the future.

A combination of rowlock brick arches and timbrel vaults support the roof, made of stone slabs from Montjuïc. The upper part of the roof will be added later, when the domes have been raised and flat surfaces to allow the highest points of the church to be completed are no longer required.

Work on the roofs. >

Roof of the cloister.

Details of the construction.

The sacristies and individual chapels

The sacristies are set at each corner of the building and in the central area behind the apse. These important elements have yet to be built and stand out from the continuity of the cloister which runs around the church.

'The paraboloid is the father of all geometry', Gaudí used to say. He designed these cupola structures which occupy the north and west corners of the cloister covered by lanterns and dedicated to the 'ember days' of observance in Autumn and Advent. The groined vaults and large parabolic cones of the extrados, made of bare brick, are extremely graceful and will be decorated with Venetian *trencadís* mosaic combined with small porphyry pinnacles.

Gaudí made in-depth studies of the sacristies, which also proved to be useful as experiments for the construction of the domes dedicated to Jesus Christ and the Virgin Mary.

Model of the Chapel of the Assumption.

< Plaster model of the sacristy.

The Baptistery and the Chapel of the Sacrament occupy opposite corners of the main façade. A rough sketch by Gaudí shows their structure supported by central columns and surrounded by the cloister. Externally similar to the sacristies, these corners also contain small chapels and lanterns dedicated to the ember days of Lent and Pentecost.

The bell-towers and domes

The first bell-tower, the tower of St. Barnabus, was completed on 30 November 1925. Gaudí expressed his delight at seeing how 'that lance joined the heavens with the earth'. He added: 'the parabolic form of these vertical bell-towers is the union of gravity with light'. This was the start of the new architecture which he left us, entirely built by Gaudí himself. The other three were completed by architect Domènec Sugrañes, the master's successor and collaborator, who left the Nativity façade almost finished. Twelve bell-towers are included in the plans, reaching heights of from 98 to 120 metres over the floor of the church. On the Nativity façade are Matthew, Judas, Simon and Barnabus, on the Passion, James, Bartholomew, Thomas and Philip, and on the Glory, Andrew, Peter, Paul and James. The transept and apse are crowned with a further six domes dedicated to Jesus Christ, the Four Evangelists and Our Lady. The highest of these will culminate in a 170-metre high cross. During the day, this will sparkle with mosaics, and at night will emit shafts of light over the other bell-towers, seeming to bring the whole city under its protection, in enactment of the words of Jesus, 'I am the light' (John, 8, 12).

Gaudí worked long and hard on the terminations of the bell-towers. In the model presented at the Paris Exhibition in 1910, the solution he planned was quite different from what we see today: so-called 'pineapple beacons' were to receive and project rays of symbolic light. Lack of re-

Terminations of the bell-towers.

sources, however, ensured that Gaudí had more time to compose the geometrical figures symbolising the Apostles, with the episcopal attributes of the Ring, the Mitre, the Crosier and the Cross. The almost 25-metre high terminations begin with letters spelling out 'Hosanna Excelsis', in ascending order in an enveloping hexagonal, separated by channels formed by dihedral angles decorated with pyramid-shaped encircling dark green glazed fired brick.

On top of these rise geometric forms with gold and silver Venetian mosaic on a red background, converging at the confluence of the octahedron and a perforated

Terminations of the side and central naves and the pinnacles of the apse.

Access stairway to the choir gallery of the Glory Façade.

sphere, housing reflectors and representing the episcopal Ring. A triangular pyramid-shaped trunk curves round, forming the Crosier, whilst two diverging curvilinear squares represent the Mitre and the Cross.

The bell-towers emerge from the mass of the three great doors in each façade, dedicated to the Theological Virtues. They

< *Bell-towers and Eucharistic symbols of bread and wine.*

Bell-towers of the Passion Façade.

Interior of one of the bell-towers. >

have a double gallery inside which ascends a helicoidal staircase, rising amidst the chiaroscuro of the ribs of vertical stone and the vertically ascending inclined planes. The interior space was to be hung with tubular and traditional bells, designed by Gaudí to ring out across the city.

Stairway of the apse.

Stairway of the bell-towers on the Passion Façade.

Stairway of the bell-towers on the Nativity Façade.

Detail of the narrow stairway.

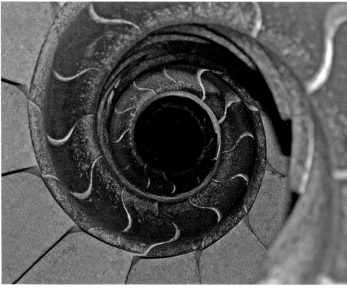

School of the Sagrada Família.

Detail.

The School

The general plan of the church envisaged that part of the semi-basement would be used for imparting professional training. As Gaudí said: 'beside the Church, people will receive education and culture'. The riots of July 1909 known as 'Setmana Tràgica' (tragic week) lead to the provisional construction of the parish school. Here, Gaudí demonstrated his enormous architectural ability with both great simplicity and surprising complexity. Inside, inclined vertical partition walls support beams that sustain an undulating concave-convex roof, shaped to collect water and also to provide greater structural strength. The roof span over the three classrooms was divided in half so that standard section and length planks could be used. This is why steel poles and a main beam, running the entire length of the building, divide it into a rectangle of 20 x 10 metres in perimeter.

Le Corbusier's visit to the works of the church and the sketch he made mythified this construction. The fire caused by hotheaded revolutionaries in July 1936 destroyed the school, and it was rebuilt with some modifications by the architect Francesc Quintana.

School. A combination of conoids forms the roof and façades.

Because it obstructed the building of the church naves it had to be moved a few metres to enable its reconstruction based on the original. This has allowed this small sample of timbrel vault technology using conoids on the roof and outside walls to be retained by transferring all the existing original elements, letting us admire the genius of Gaudí beside the great monument formed by the church.

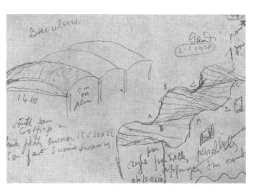

Sketch by Le Corbusier made during his visit to Barcelona.

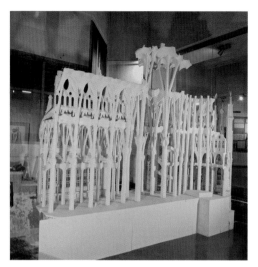

Plaster model of the structure (scale: 1:25).

The Structure

Gaudí's first plans for the church were inspired by the Gothic style. He stressed the verticality of the elements, as can be seen in his sketch of the entire building seen from the apse ('El Propagador', 1891).

The extraordinary and intelligent solution of completing the Nativity façade with the opportunities this afforded for obtaining a large donation, extended the time required to draw up the overall plan for the church. The economic precariousness of the project was actually useful, in that it contributed to Gaudí devoting the last twelve years of his life to making the Sagrada Família the most important architectural achievement of the 20th century in structural terms. In his search for pres-

sure curves and wish for them to coincide with architectural forms, he decided to incline his columns, identifying the mechanical and architectural organism in each element. He therefore ramified the columns from a given height upwards, so as to spread the dead weights of the vaults by multiplying the active resistance elements. The result is an arboreal, balanced, light structure which considerably reduces the great masses of construction required by a Gothic cathedral. Moreover, Gaudí planned to use reinforced concrete to reduce the need for costly scaffolding to support the weight of the building until a projected structure could be balanced.

Furthermore, Gaudí selected the strongest natural materials to support the heavy loads borne by the other domes and stone roofs planned. These also served to fireproof the building while their loads helped to absorb seismic tremors.

Nowadays, using computers and with contributions from architects Joan Margarit, Carles Buxadé and Josep Gómez Serrano, the feasibility of Gaudí's original project has been fully demonstrated.

Mock-up made by calculating and projecting the chapel of the Colònia Güell from photographs by a team led by Professor Frei Otto.

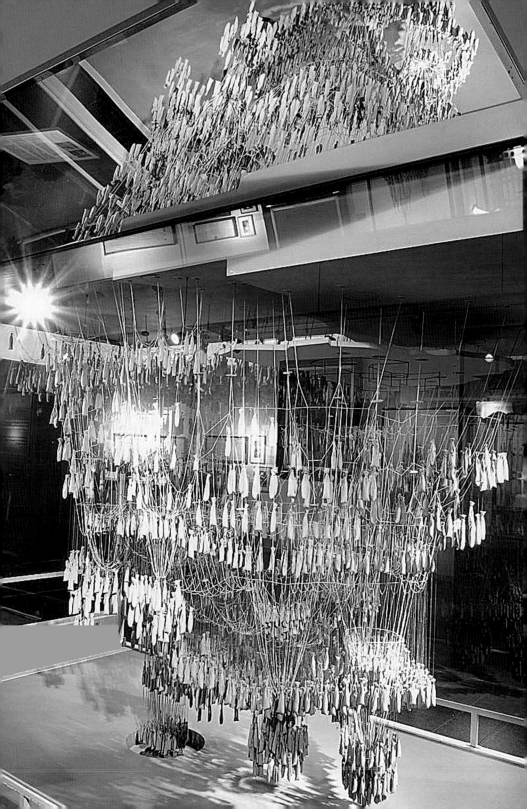

Branched upper part of the columns.

The geometric modelling

Gaudí was fully aware that he would never see the completion of the church his creative genius had projected. He had very clear ideas about the synthesis of structure and form he wished to achieve, however. His knowledge of curved forms generated by straight lines, that is, ruled surfaces - hyperbolic paraboloids, helicoids, hyperboloids and conoids - and their structural and plastic potential as regards lighting and sound, and all the beauty he had observed in nature, led Gaudí to leave them volumetrically resolved, clearly defined and easily to apply in the future.

Because the last twelve years of his life were devoted exclusively to the Sagrada Família, Gaudí was able to study and produce a series of 1:10 and 1:25 scale plaster models as the culmination of his contribution to architecture.

All the plans were burnt when Gaudí's studio was sacked by revolutionaries in July 1936, but the plaster models, though broken, survived the destruction. A close study of the pieces revealed the geometrical modelling with which he wished to define his thinking, so that the work he planned could be continued according to his design.

Knots or capitals of
the transept.

1/6	2/6	3/6	4/6	5/6	6/6	
Ø 35	Ø 70	Ø 105	Ø 140	Ø 175	Ø 210	
H 3,5m	H 7m	H 10,5m	H 14m	H 17,5m	H 21m	
CLAUSTRE PASIÓ	NAU LATERAL	NAU LATERAL I ABSIS 1/2	NAU LATERAL 2/3	TRANSEPTE	CREUER	
1/6		Ø 105.00	Ø 140.00	Ø 175.00	Ø 210.00	COLUMNES INFERIORS
1	1	2	2	2	3	
	Ø 70.00 Ø 52.50	H 30m Ø 52.50 Ø 70.00 157.50 3/12 3/12 52.50 52.50 H 30m	H 30m Ø 52.50 87.50 87.50 Ø 87.50 5/12 H 45m	H 30m Ø 87.50 Ø 70.00 87.50 87.50 Ø 87.50 5/12 H 45m	H 45m Ø 105.00 Ø 122.50 Ø 140.00	COLUMNES SUPERIORS
	TEMPLE DE LA SAGRADA FAMÍLIA SÈRIE DE LES COLUMNES			H 60m	7/12 Ø 105.00	COLUMNES VOLTES Escala 1 : 100

Chart showing the proportions of different models of columns.

These simple proportions are repeated throughout the Sagrada Família, based on multiples and divisions of twelve, in common use in Catalonia since the Middle Ages. The intercolumn of 7.5 metres, repeated twelve times, equals the 90 metres of the length of the interior of the church, producing the following series:

90	82.5	75	67.5	60	52.5	45	37.5	30	22.5	15	7.5
12	11	10	9	8	7	6	5	4	3	2	1

This is one of the many mathematical series forming the measurements of the church which, taken together, weave the immense spider's web which modulates it geometrically. The convergence of structure and form through geometry allows us to obtain the same results as Gaudí and, of course, many of those he could not materially resolve, but which are easy to deduce thanks to the geometrical modelling he conceived. From his observations of nature, Gaudí has left us highly detailed plaster models of his 'new architecture'. A living architecture in which life is shown with colour and movement, based on double-curve geometric shapes. Research has allowed us to use computers to cut the stone of these surfaces, while remaining absolutely faithful to Gaudí's plans.

The Symbolism

'The entire Church of the Sagrada Família is a hymn of praise to God intoned by Humanity and whose every stone is a verse sung in a clear, strong, harmonious voice', writes Puig Boada. Gaudí was determined that this was to be the church of an entire people, a hymn to the Trinity of God.

From the outside, the Sagrada Família building symbolises the Church, Jesus Christ and the faithful, represented by Mary, the Apostles and the Saints. The twelve bell-towers represent the Apostles, these first bishops of the Church, the voices which exhort the faithful, extolled witnesses to the revelation received.

Inside, the columns supporting the vaults and roof also represent the Apostles and the local churches with their saints. In other words, the whole world, from the Catalan dioceses to those of the five continents, as well as celestial Jerusalem, the mystical city of peace which the Lamb of God has won for us.

Gaudí said that the naves and the vaults would be 'Like a forest. Light will enter in abundance through windows placed at different heights. It will be possible to follow the main daily prayers (the *Te Deum*, the *Miserere*, the *Benedictus* and the *Magnificat*) from the inscriptions on the handrails of the choir and the triforiums'.

Among the columns encircling the transept and apse dedicated to the Apostles and the Evangelists those of the Apostles

Alpha, omega: the beginning and the end.

A tortoise and a turtle supporting columns: immutability in time.

The centurion Longinus on the Passion Façade.

Magic square or kamea from the era of Christ.

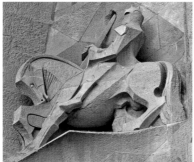

The baldachin of the Sagrada Família is a metallic heptagon of some five metres in diametre, from which hang bunches of grapes (glass), vine leaves (copper) and ears of corn (varnished white wood with copper nails), with laterals lined with parchment and covered with tapestry.

Saint Thomas the Apostle.

Peter and Paul are particularly important, uniting the triumphal arch with the Calvary, the Virgin Mary, the Crucifixion and St. John. The representation of the Trinity will be completed by the image of the Eternal Father, which will be seen on entering the church in its place in the dome of the apse, with a seven-branched lamp symbolising the Holy Spirit. The inscription of the Hymn of Glory and the hanging canopy which protects the altar will focus the attention of worshippers. In the triforium on the side of the Passion façade is the Virgin Mary, surrounded by angels with the attributes of the Litany. On the Nativity façade is St. Joseph with the attributes of his trade. Along with the crucifix at the altar, he completes the representation of the Holy Family.

Mother of God.

Saint Joseph.

Plasticity

For any work of architecture to be considered beautiful, its elements must be appropriately located and fitting in dimensions, form and colour.

Nature

Gaudí's plasticity is based on his study of nature, and is expressed in forms and colours. We have already seen how Gaudí commented on his learning from nature as follows: 'This tree, next to my workshop, is my master'. Observing it, he drew conclusions which he put into practice in his projects. The use of natural forms, of flora and fauna, is frequent throughout his work and in many of the details of the church of the Sagrada Família. It is from this study of nature that his abstract geometrical forms are derived, the result of combinations of convergences, and new forms which had never before been used in architecture.

Eucharistic symbols of bread and wine.

Detail of snail-shaped gargoyles.

Composition of stars.

Balcony with the symbols of Jesus, Joseph and Mary; the crown of thorns, the plane and the jar.

Form

Natural forms are present even in the capitals in the crypt and the gargoyles and bell-towers of the apse. On the Nativity façade, the human figure, plants and animals are present, expressing the Mystery of the Nativity, with all that surrounds the childhood of Jesus. They are also found in the windows, in the sculptural motifs representing fruits from the different seasons of the year. Geometrical forms based on simple elements and drawings became increasingly complicated as Gaudí became more familiar with the study and use of curved surfaces. He first made use of paraboloids, then of hyperboloids and helicoloids, producing a great outburst

Details of the façade, showing the exquisite nature and diversity of the work.

of theoretical and formal innovation. The columns, windows and vaults which Gaudí planned in the later years of his life are the exponent of an extraordinary work of research and study. This is also true of the bell-towers, the domes and other elements.

Colour

Colour is another important element in Gaudí's architecture. In the church of the Sagrada Família, the terminations of the bell-towers are the finest examples of the results that could be obtained from his use of colour. A model demonstrating Gaudí's ideas for the Nativity façade on a scale of 1:25 was made for the Paris Exhibition in 1910, but was unfortunately destroyed in 1936. Following this model, however, some of Gaudí's theories were applied in the chapel in the Colonia Güell and other works.

Gaudí planned to use Venetian mosaic, which would make the colour a lasting sign of life, instead of ephemeral as it would be with ceramic *trencadis* mosaic.

To be able to express Gaudí's ideas an artist sufficiently versed in the potential of stained glass was brought in. Joan Vila Grau has made most of the windows in the apse and both transepts, and will continue to do the same in the naves.

Sculptor Etsuro Sotoo has also completed figures on the Nativity façade and the terminations of the lateral façades from Gaudí's original models, with fruit and the Eucharistic symbols of bread and wine.

Stained glass windows, lights, monstrance and other examples of the play of light and colour.

Acoustics and lighting

Gaudí had studied acoustic issues and experimented with the tubular bells he installed in the elongated hollow sections of the bell-towers, as well as with the organs which were to fill the naves with resounding music. There are singing galleries on either side of the nave, in the interior of the rear section of the Glory façade and above the ambulatory in the apse, where there is space for the children's choir, accommodating a total of 1,500 choristers. With priests around the altar, Gaudí felt certain that people would take part in services, showing himself in this as in many other questions, in advance of the 2nd Vatican Council's decisions regarding the liturgy. Light, entering harmoniously through the

The "tetramorphs" give light to the crossing.

Organ impregnated with light from the windows.

The lighting in the interior of the Basílica is harmonious and soft. >

great high windows, diffused by the new geometrical surfaces, will prevent excessive contrast, lending greater visibility to the decorated surfaces. Spotlights placed at the mouths of the hyperboloids of the vaults will add diffused lighting at night. The light from the stained glass windows and the lights suspended from the hyperboloids on the ellipsoids of the knots and the capitals of the columns in the central nave, will all add to the polychromatic luminosity. As Gaudí explained, 'The church will be full of light, with beautiful filtering effects, combining the light coming in from the domes with that from the glass of the high windows. All this will illuminate the polychromy of the interior'.

Confessional.

Portable pulpit.

Liturgical objects

Gaudí planned the altars, objects and furniture for worship at the church crypt, instructing us liturgically through the dignity and quality of each item. The benches, sacristy cupboards, pulpit and confessionals, the candelabra and sideboards, the ceremonial chairs, lights and chandeliers, with the candelabra and lectern and candlestick for the large Easter candle.

The baldaquin of Mallorca Cathedral is one extraordinary element which Gaudí was not able to complete. But its description was available, and this has been followed for the Sagrada Família as far as possible. Only the measurements and location of the altar were known. Once again, chance played its part, and the arrival of an exceptional block of stone intended for the tambours of the porphyry columns in the transept offered another solution: of reserving it, keeping the chisel

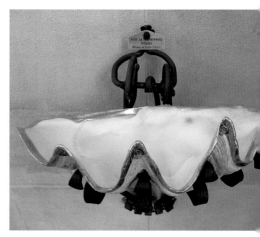

Font with holy water.

marks and polishing the flat cut surface. In a way this option recalled the shapes of the basalt columns which Gaudí wished to leave just as they came from the quarry, in the crypt of the Colonia Güell.

Ornament cupboard.

Ceremonial chair.

Most of the design of the crypt benches has been retained, but the presbytery choir stalls have been simplified.

The organ will be completed once the building work is finished. The instrument is suitable for accompaniment, with almost 30 registers and almost 2000 pipes in the centre and side of the ambulatory, until in future one with the proper height (30 m) can be installed where Gaudí wished.

Small elements will be missing - symbols and dedications which the Master wished to be added to the catechism that he wanted to reach the people.

Tenebrae candelabra.

Present state and immediate future

At present, 4,500 m² of the church has been roofed, two façades - the Nativity and the Passion – are almost complete, and the western sacristy is about to be built for use for parish services. The next task will be erecting the central part of the transept, along with the extension of the Museum and its access at street level from Carrer Mallorca. We will also soon see the pediment of the Passion, with the patriarchs and prophets and the empty tomb, witness to the resurrection. Elevators will take visitors up into the vaults in the transept, and work will continue on the baptistry, to finish the transept with the cross above the church, if all goes well, and within this first quarter-century, the bell-towers of the Glory façade.

But some problems have not yet been overcome, problems that had not been anticipated but which have been affecting the works for a decade, ranging from the tunnel for the high-speed train to the ordination of the surrounding area.

The faithful and other friends of the Expiatory Church of the Sagrada Família form the spiritual support which is carrying forward the idea, and the works continue to advance with contributions of all kinds, great and small, gathered in every day.

Aerial views of the state of construction (2010).

Another view of the state of the works.

We could add to this the selfless devotion of many of the people who work on the site: technicians, plasterers, sculptors, stone cutters, mechanics, carpenters, etc. The administration is austere, enabling the pace of the work to adapt to the income received in the form of donations of all types. Above all, from the entrance fees of the millions of visitors who come here, just as Gaudí prophesied: 'People will come from all over the world to see what we are doing'.

Technically, the most modern methods are being used: computers to calculate the structure or to work the stone, quality control of the stone and concrete used, and new machinery and technologies created to enhance the work and safety in the construction.

Over ten years ago a crane was installed to reach heights of 140 m. Now we are already working there and considering the next step, although no-one knows what new technologies will be available. Many people ask us when it will be finished. This is a difficult question to answer, as it depends on donations received, but there is a programme for the present and another for the near future which are gradually putting into place the plans of the Foundation's Board of Trustees. Gaudí took between 40 and 50 years to build

Palm Sunday at the Sagrada Família.

one façade, along with the crypt and the walls of the apse. There followed the trauma of the Spanish Civil War, which paralysed work for 20 years. The generation of those who knew him, his direct disciples, took 20 years to build the Passion façade. As I wrote a few years ago, we can expect the vaults to be closed in the early part of the 21st century.

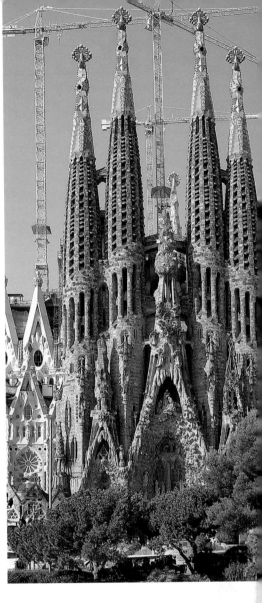

The works are largely funded by the entrance fees of the many people who wish to look around the building and to collaborate in its construction.

Lovers of the church

Joan Maragall.

President Prat de la Riba and Bishop Reig listen to Gaudí's explanations.

'The church of the Sagrada Família is being built by the people and is a reflection of their way of being. In the Sagrada Família, everything is providential', Gaudí used often to repeat, adding that this would be 'the church of today's Catalonia'. The poet Joan Maragall, a great friend of Gaudí, was the first to realise the transcendence of the master's work, and was his earliest supporter in the press.

But then a series of events threatened to wipe the church from the face of the earth: the school was destroyed, Gaudí's entire studio disappeared, though not his spirit. The centenary of the architect's birth in 1952 re-awakened interest in the project. Until then, no art history book had mentioned his work, and no eminent historians had even heard of him. With the controversy over whether the work should continue or not, the silence which had surrounded the last years of Gaudí's life began to be broken down and the arguments re-examined. But the people continued their faith in him, and alms and donations were arriving. The collection, taken on one Sunday every year, received increasing support. 'This work lies in the hands of God and the will of the people', Gaudí used to say. The Catalans have responded generously, and have fallen in love with the growing church, 'their' church. Right up to the present, when the image of the church of the Sagrada Família has come to symbolise the city of Barcelona.

Narcís Jubany.

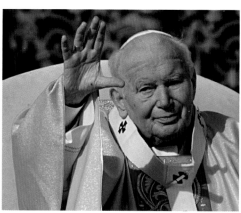

Visit of Pope John Paul II in 1982.

It was Narcís Jubany, Cardenal-Archbishop of Barcelona, who took the decision to start the construction of the naves due to the continuous donation of alms, these mostly humble but numerous expressions of the popular will.

UNESCO declared Gaudí's work to be Heritage of Mankind not long after the 150th anniversary of his birth.

Shortly after Gaudí's death, a young Japanese architect, Kenji Imai, arrived in Barcelona. He did not meet the master, but was so deeply impressed by his work that he made it widely known in Japan. He even dared to build the cathedral in Nagasaki following the ideas his study of Gaudí's work had inspired. Since then, Japanese people come to see his works because

he architect Kenji Imai and an example of Gaudí's influence on his work.

Walter Gropius.

Le Corbusier.

they know him to be one of the great masters of modern architecture.

In the 1950s, the German architect Gropius visited the Chapel of the Colonia Güell, staying there for over an hour in silent contemplation of such a marvel. Le Corbusier reproduced the church school in a sketch in 1927 after his first visit to Barcelona, later writing about Gaudí that he is 'the Builder of the turn of the century'.

In Paris in 1961, in the exhibition 'Origins of the 20th Century' Gaudí's values, which had not been understood in 1910, were finally recognised. In Italy, in Britain, in Holland, in Germany and in New Zealand, all over the world, Gaudí's originality was at last acclaimed, and the architect became considered one of the greatest exponents in the entire history of art. His Holiness Pope John Paul II took in the Sagrada Família as part of his visit to Barcelona

and since then no visiting figure from the world of politics, art or science has failed to visit this renowned monument. To visit a church under construction. An unusual experience indeed. And finally, on the seventh of November 2010, the Holy Father dedicated the church, opening it for permanent worship.

Why this great influx of visitors? Today, contemporary art has found a Christian expression in this surprising architecture. Benedict XVI has written about the encounter of Art and Faith. The response is not easy, but the building of this church dedicated to Jesus, Mary and Joseph, the Holy Family of Nazareth, is the expression of the solidarity of faith and hope, founded on love which, with its invocation of the Father, God the Creator, is a symbol of the fraternity of all mankind.

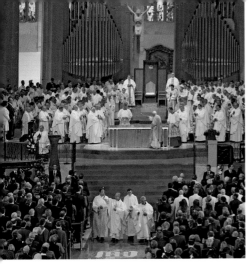

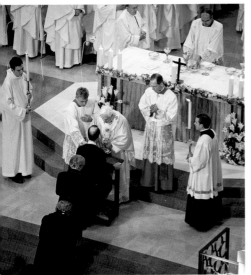

Visit of Pope Benedict XVI and dedication of the Sagrada Família..

CHRONOLOGY OF THE BASILICA OF THE SAGRADA FAMÍLIA

1876	Josep Maria Bocabella founds the 'Spiritual Association of the Devotees of St. Joseph' which will become the church's promoter.
1882	First stone laid. Project by architect Francisco de Paula de Villar.
1883	**Antoni Gaudí takes over as architect of the church.**
1889	The crypt is finished.
1890	Drawing up of the first overall design.
1892	Work begins on the Nativity façade.
1894	Apse façade completed.
1899	Completion of the Rose Tree Door in the cloister.
1909	Building of the parish school.
1910	Exhibition in Paris of the mock-up of the Nativity façade.
1917	Project for the Passion façade, with the monument to Bishop Torres i Bages.
1923	Final design for central and side naves, and roofs in 1:10 and 1:25 scale plaster models.
1925	30 November. First bell-tower (Saint Barnabus), 100 metres high, is finished.
1926	**Antoni Gaudí dies in an accident on 10 June.**
1930	The four bell-towers of the Nativity façade are completed.
1936	**Spanish Civil War. Profanation and destruction in the church. Gaudí's studio destroyed.**
1940	Restoration of the crypt and plaster models.
1954	Work begins on the Passion façade.
1977	**The four bell-towers of the Passion Façade are completed.**
1978	Work begins on the fronts of the naves.
1986-90	Foundations of the naves. First sculptures for the Passion façade.
1995	Construction of the side nave vaults.
1997-98	Construction of the central nave.
2000	Work begins on the vaults in the transept, the crossing and the foundations of the Glory façade.
2002	Transfer and restoration of the school building.
2005	Work begins on the Evangelist bell-towers and the transept vaults. Apse columns 30 m. Work begins on the choir gallery on the Glory façade.
2010	**Dedication of the church.**